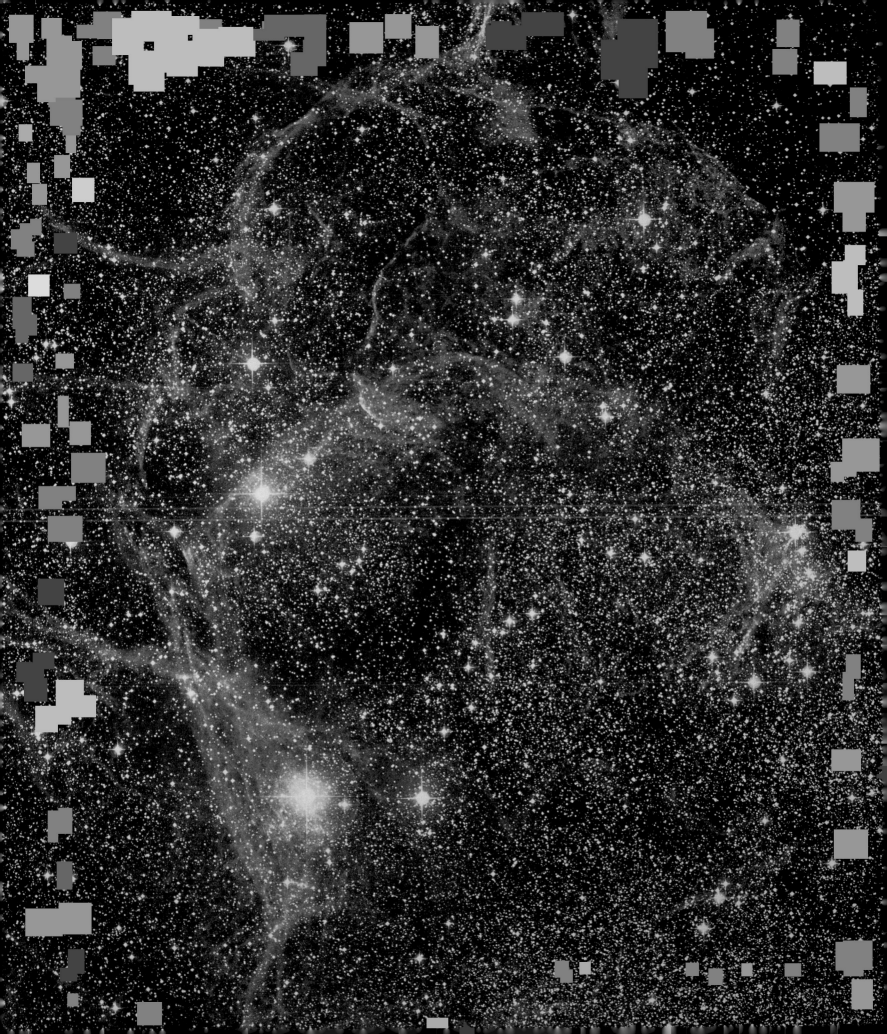

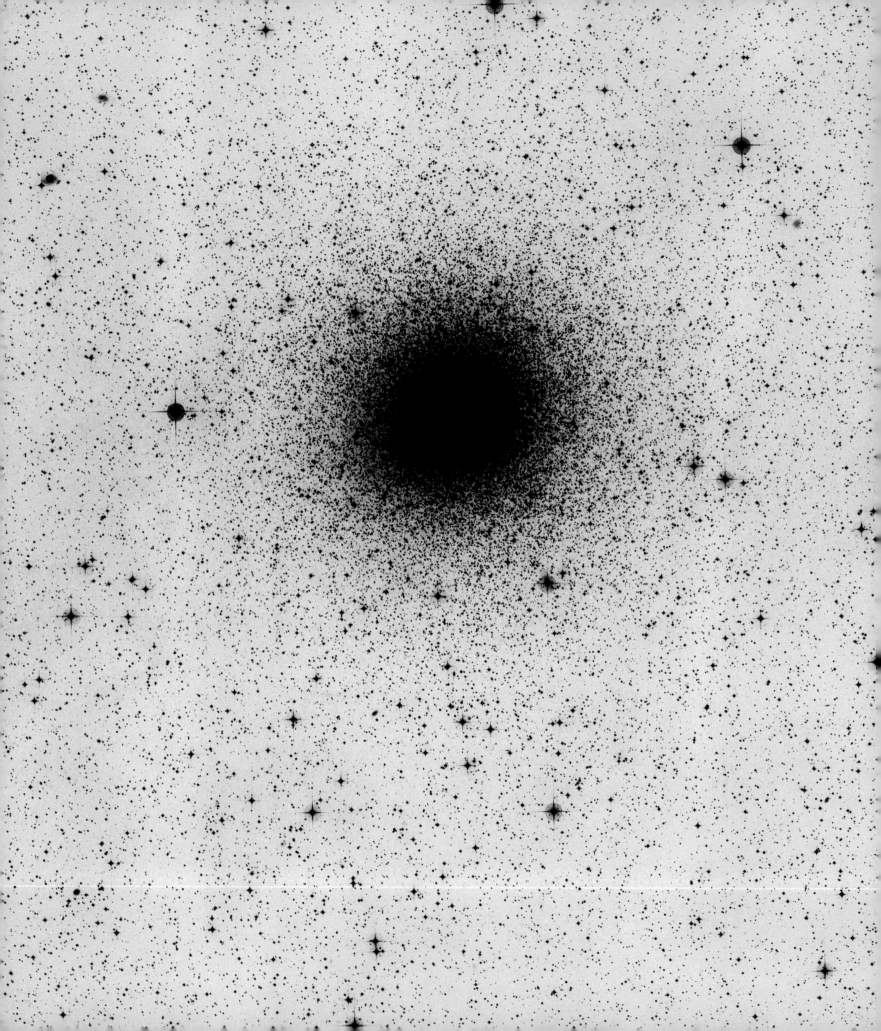

STARS

MICHAEL GEORGE

CREATIVE EDUCATION INC.

Designed by Rita Marshall
with the help of Thomas Lawton

© 1991 Creative Education, Inc.
123 South Broad Street,
Mankato, Minnesota 56001

Photography by Anglo-Australian
Observatory, Frank Rossotto, Hale
Observatories, Holiday Film, Lick
Observatory, Palomar Observatories,
Peter Arnold, Photo Researchers,
Photri, Royal Observatory—
Edinburgh, and Uniphoto

Library of Congress
Cataloging-in-Publication Data

George, Michael, 1964–
Stars / by Michael George.
Summary: Discusses the nature of
stars, how they are formed and
change, and the different kinds.
ISBN 0-88682-400-1
1. Stars—Juvenile literature.
2. Astronomy—Juvenile literature.
[1. Stars. 2. Astronomy.] I. Title.
QB801.7.G46   1991   90-22654
623.8—dc20   CIP
                          AC

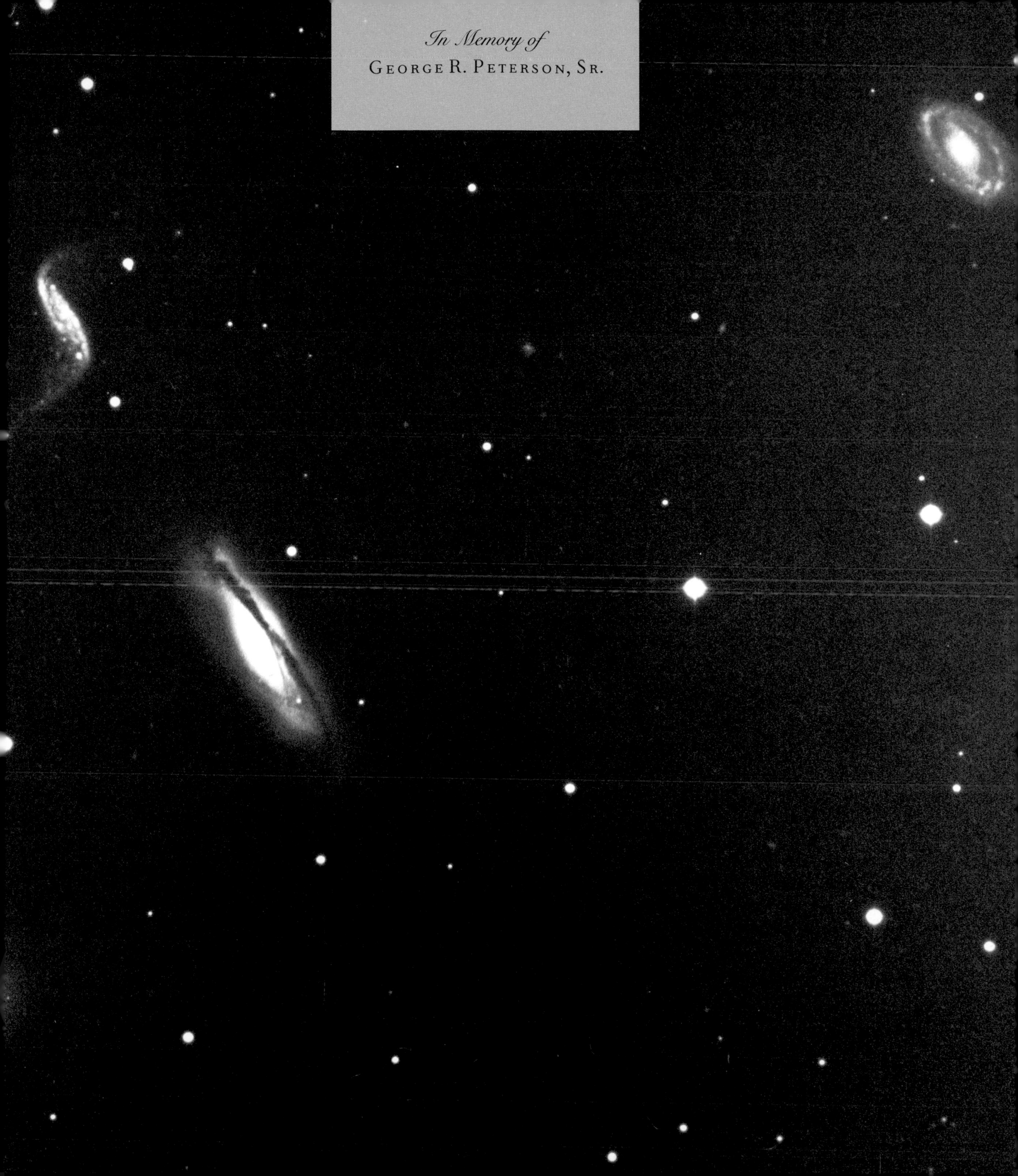

Since the very beginnings of humankind, we have been fascinated by the stars. Twinkling in the dark night sky, *The Stars* evoke questions that beg to be answered; what is a star, where are they located, and what is their significance for life on Earth? In the past few centuries, scientists have answered many of these questions. The answers reveal the intricate workings of our universe and the delicate balance of life on Earth.

Page 6: Open star cluster.
Page 7: Our galaxy, the Milky Way.

Many people think that stars are visible only at night. One star, however, can be seen only during the day. That is the star we call *The Sun*. The Sun is an enormous ball of hot, glowing gases. It is large enough to hold over one million Earths, and hot enough to warm our planet and light our sky. Without the Sun, the Earth would be frozen, the sky would be black, and life would not exist on our planet.

❧

Despite its unique appearance and importance to life on Earth, the Sun is just an ordinary star. It is no different from the stars that are visible every night. The Sun appears to be bigger and brighter than all the other stars simply because it is the closest star to the Earth. Like the Sun, all stars are extremely large, hot balls of glowing gas.

Page 8: The night sky.
Page 9: Our Sun.

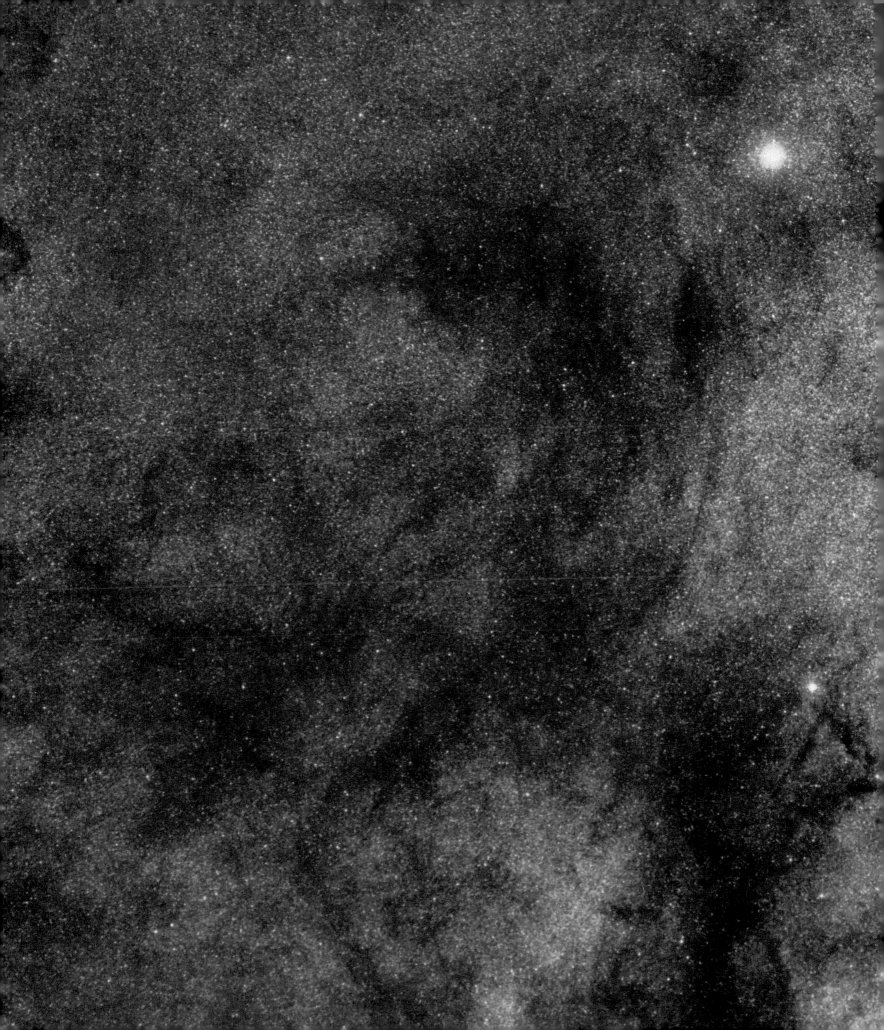

On dark, moonless nights we can see about 2000 stars in the sky. However, there are countless other stars that cannot be seen. In fact, many of the specks of light in the night sky are actually two stars. The stars in these pairs, called *Binary Stars,* circle around each other in space. Most binary stars appear to be single stars simply because they are so far away from the Earth.

There are also many specks of light in the night sky that are actually three, four, or even more stars. These groups of stars are called multiple star systems. Some star systems, called *Globular Clusters,* may contain millions of stars that are visible only with powerful telescopes.

Pages 10-11: *The center of our galaxy.*
Page 11: *A globular cluster.*

The largest star systems in the universe are called *Galaxies*. Our Solar System, which includes the Sun, the Earth, and the other eight planets, belongs to the Milky Way galaxy. If you look into the nighttime sky, you can see part of *The Milky Way*. The Galaxy looks like a huge, hazy cloud stretching across the sky.

The Milky Way.

13

The Milky Way is only a faint glow because the stars are very far away. A common telescope reveals that this hazy cloud is a collection of billions of stars. Scientists estimate that the Milky Way galaxy contains 200 billion stars. If you counted one star every second, it would take 6000 years to count all the stars in our galaxy.

Although it is difficult to comprehend all the stars just in our own galaxy, the Milky Way is not the only galaxy in the universe. Peering between the stars in our galaxy, scientists can see other galaxies sprinkled throughout space. Scientists estimate that there are 100 billion *Galaxies* in the universe, each containing an average of 100 billion stars. In all, there are as many stars in the universe as there are grains of sand on the Earth.

As we have learned, of all the billions upon billions of stars in the universe, *the Sun* is the closest star to the Earth. However, the Sun is still about 93 million miles from Earth. If we traveled in the fastest spaceship toward the Sun, it would take many years to reach its surface.

Pages 14-15: The Andromeda Galaxy.

The light that we see from the Sun travels 187,000 miles every second, or nearly 700 million miles per hour. That is much faster than any spaceship has ever gone. In fact, nothing in the universe can travel as fast as a beam of light.

Although light from the Sun travels incredibly fast, it still takes some time for it to reach the Earth. The light that we see from the Sun has been traveling through space for just over eight minutes. These rays of light are actually images of the Sun. Therefore, we do not see the Sun as it is at this moment; we see an image of the Sun as it was about eight minutes ago.

Our Sun's light.

The stars we see in the night sky are millions of times farther away than the Sun. The light we see from the star closest to the Sun, called *Alpha Centauri,* left the surface over four years ago. Therefore, we see Alpha Centauri as it was four years ago. Other stars are so far away that we see them as they were thousands of years ago, when our ancestors lived in caves. Some stars are even farther away than this. We see these stars as they were before life existed on the Earth, or before the Earth had even formed.

Our planet changed drastically in the time it took the light from distant stars to reach it. Similarly, the stars have also changed. In fact, some of the stars we see in the sky may not even exist any longer. This is because stars, like people, are born and eventually die. During their lives, stars change in re-markable ways.

Many types of stars.

A star is born in a giant cloud of gas and dust called a nebula. *Nebulae,* the plural form of nebula, consist mainly of tiny hydrogen atoms, but contain other microscopic particles as well. Within some nebulae are small, dense balls of dust and gas, called *Globules.* Just as Earth's gravity pulls objects toward the ground, a globule's gravity pulls dust and gas toward its surface. Bit by bit, the globule grows in size. After millions of years the globule is a dense, heavy globe, hundreds of times larger than the Earth.

Two Globular Clusters.

As the globule continues to grow, matter in the globule is packed closer and closer together. With the pressure constantly increasing, the temperature at the center of the globe begins to soar. Eventually, the core becomes hot enough to set off a chain of nuclear explosions. In a process called *Nuclear Fusion,* hydrogen atoms combine to form a completely different atom called helium. Nuclear fusion releases tremendous amounts of energy, and the star begins to shine.

Different shapes of galaxies.

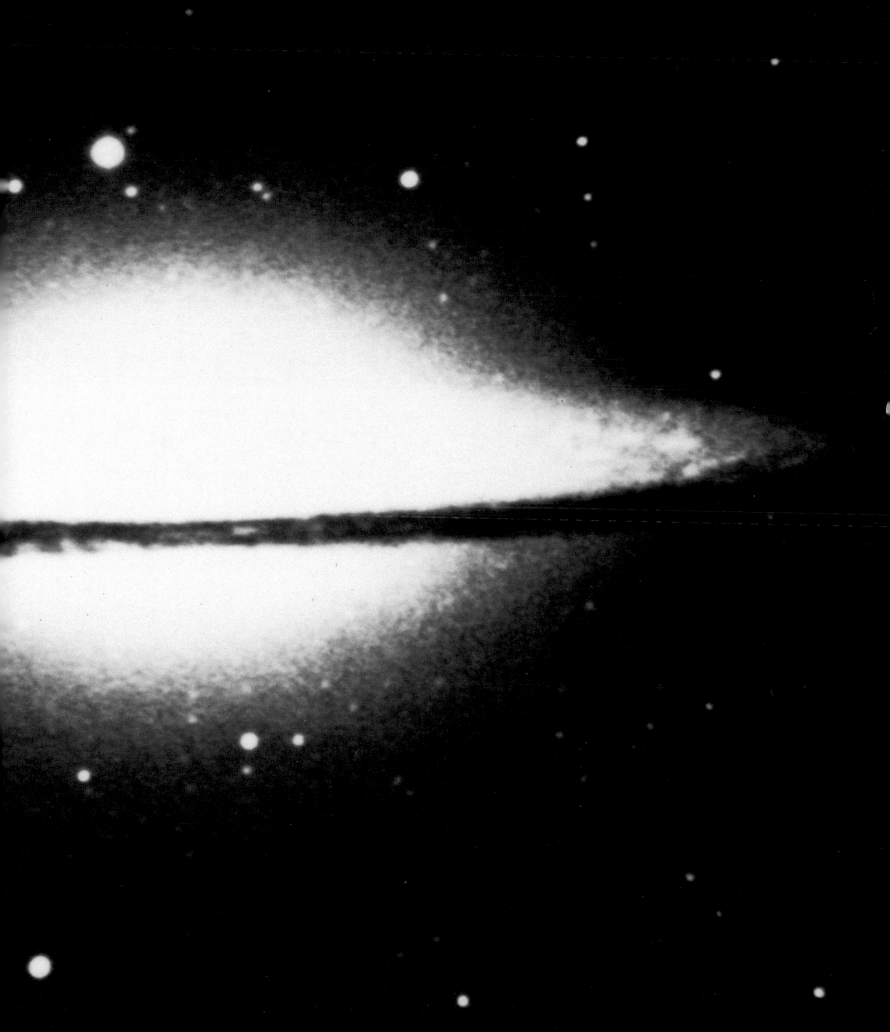

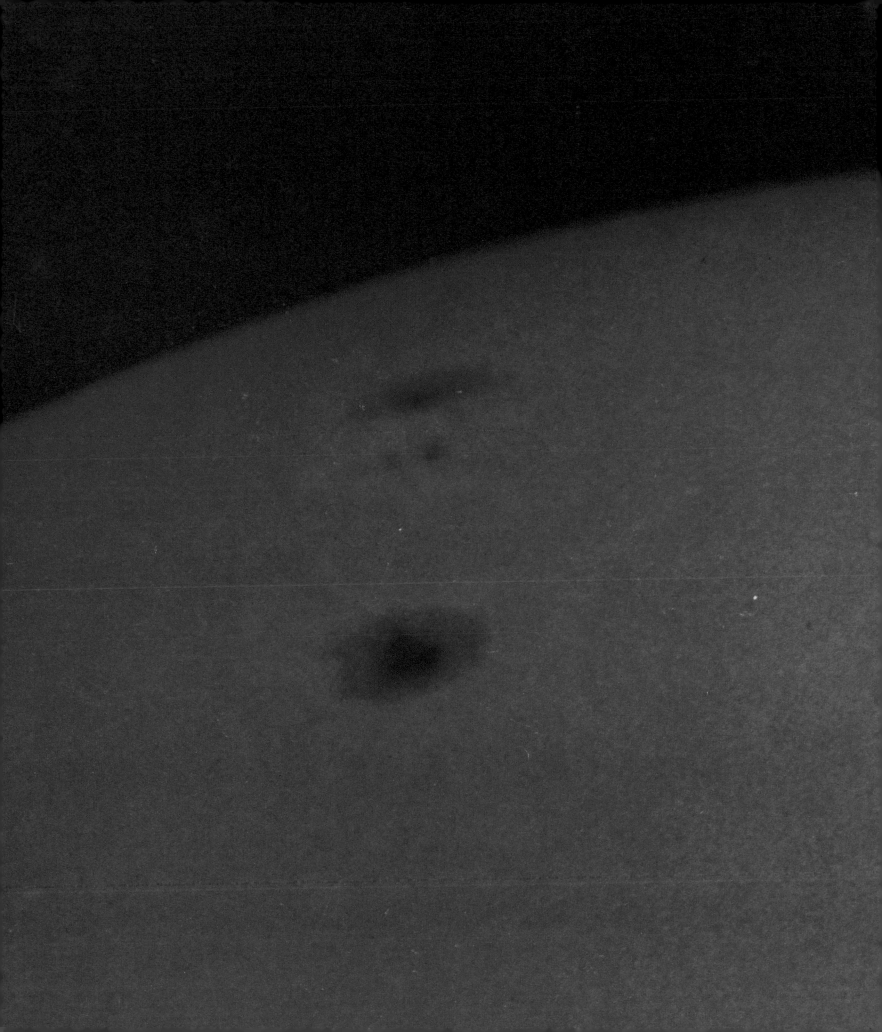

25

Once a star begins to shine, its surface churns with currents, turbulence, and gigantic waves of gas. Occasionally, thick clouds of glowing gas burst above the surface. As these blazing sheets of gas drift above the star, violent storms rage across the surface. These storms, called *Sunspots,* look like dark patches because they are thousands of degrees cooler than the rest of the star. Sometimes, sunspots erupt with violent explosions that send streams of particles and radiation far into space.

Pages 24-25: Sunspots.
Page 25: Solar Prominence.

As the surface of a star erupts with activity, nuclear fusion moves out from the center of the star toward fresh hydrogen fuel. Meanwhile, a growing core of helium ash is left behind. After about 10 billion years, most stars begin to run out of hydrogen fuel. With less energy flowing toward the surface, the star begins to contract. As the core of the star is squeezed tighter and tighter, the helium ash grows hotter and hotter. Eventually, the temperature becomes so hot that helium atoms begin to "melt" together, forming completely new atoms called *Carbon*. This releases more energy and causes the star to burst, similar to a piece of popcorn.

Our Sun.

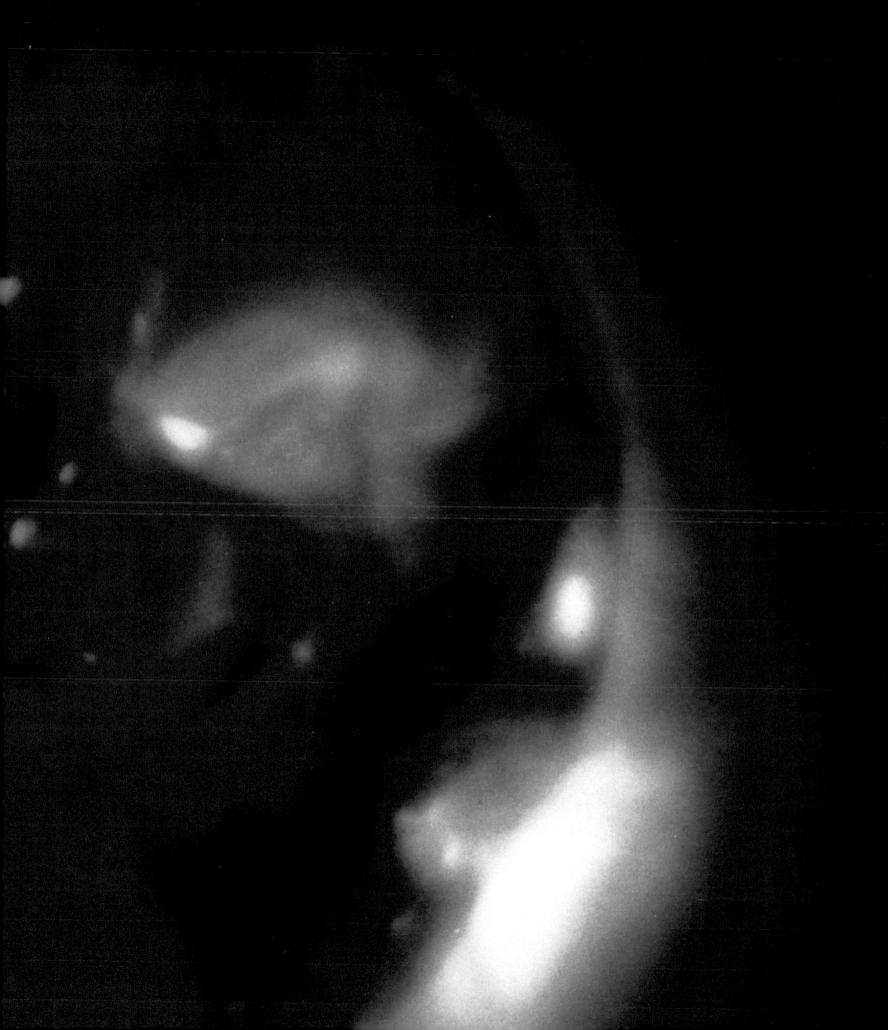

Enlarged stars such as these are called *Red Giants*. Red Giants are enormous stars, even when compared to the Sun. Most are about 40 to 50 million miles across, or about fifty times wider than the Sun. Some red giants are even larger than this. Betelgeuse, the red giant closest to the Sun, is 250 million miles across. If Betelgeuse were in the place of the Sun, it would engulf Mercury, Venus, Earth, and Mars.

Nuclear fusion cannot continue forever in the aging star. Eventually, most of the star's helium fuel is converted into carbon. Once again, the star begins to contract and temperatures begin to rise. However, carbon atoms do not ignite easily. Soon, temperatures become so hot that the star explodes and hurls its outer layers of gas into space. The expanding cloud of gases, appearing round and planetlike, is a *Planetary Nebula*.

Pages 28-29 : A Planetary Nebula.

The remaining star, now called a *White Dwarf,* shines dimly through the cloud of gas and dust. A white dwarf has no source of new energy but continues to glow simply because it is hot. Given time, the white dwarf loses heat into space and finally turns into a dark globe—a *Black Dwarf.*

Average-sized stars, such as the Sun, follow the life cycle described above. Stars that are two or three times larger than the Sun have a different fate. Under the crushing weight of a *Massive Star,* temperatures rise so high in the core that carbon atoms undergo nuclear fusion. They fuse together into a variety of other atoms. This releases additional energy for a time, but eventually, even a massive star runs out of fuel.

After all the nuclear fuel in a massive star has been used, the central core is crushed by the star's tremendous weight. This sets off a violent explosion, called a *Supernova*. A supernova makes the star millions of times brighter than normal and hurls the outer layers of the star into space. In some cases, the core of the star is also shattered. In other cases, the supernova leaves a tightly packed ball of matter called a *Neutron Star*.

A Supernova.

Neutron stars are only six to twelve miles across. Although they are very small, neutron stars contain more matter than the Sun. A single drop of a neutron star would weigh billions of pounds on Earth. Like a white dwarf, a neutron star has no source of new energy and can only cool with time.

Galaxies.

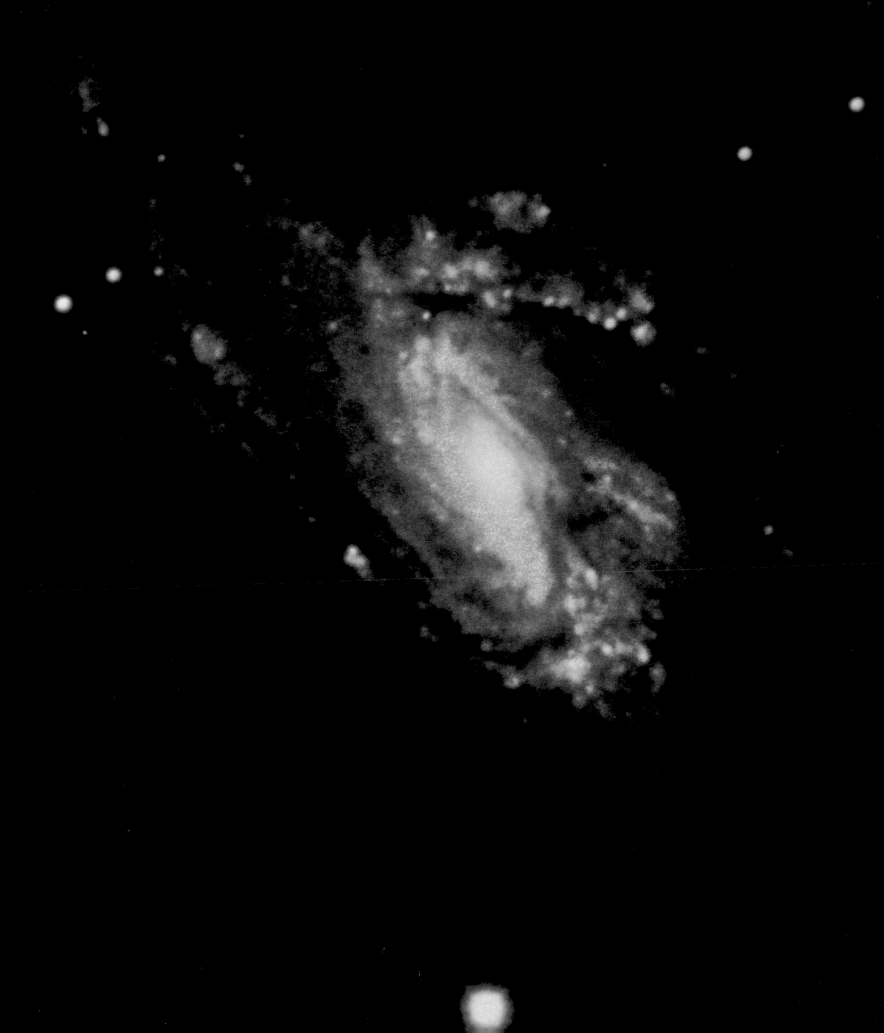

Stars that are ten or twenty times larger than the Sun end their lives in the most dramatic fashion of all. When a star this massive runs out of fuel, the tremendous gravity of the star causes it to collapse. As a star is packed tighter and tighter, the gravity of the star grows continuously stronger. Soon the gravity is so strong that the star itself is crushed out of existence. All that remains is the star's intense gravitational field, known as a *Black Hole*.

The gravity of a black hole is so strong that nothing within a certain distance can resist its pull. A black hole can engulf stars, planets, and entire solar systems. Whatever enters a black hole is lost from this universe forever; nothing, not even a beam of light, can escape.

Page 34: Spiral galaxy in Leo.

Whether they are like our Sun, or much more massive, all stars change in dramatic ways. During their long lives stars transform hydrogen into helium, helium into carbon, and carbon into a variety of other elements. In the last stages of their existence, stars hurl this newly formed matter into space. Once shed by a star, this material drifts through space as a thin cloud of gas and dust. Given time, it combines with the remains of other stars to form a nebula.

Nebulae.

As we have learned, a nebula eventually condenses into a new star. Our Sun is one of these newer stars. The nebula that condensed into the Sun also formed the Earth and the other planets in our Solar System. This nebula contained carbon, oxygen, and all the other elements we now find on Earth. These elements, created long ago in aging stars, are the basic building blocks of everything on Earth, including human beings. And so, in a way, we are all made of star dust.

Page 38: Lagoon nebula in Sagittarius.
Pages 38-39: Galaxies in space.

Stars are more than just specks of light in the sky. Every star is an enormous, evolving ball of hot, glowing gases. During their long lives, stars create the elements from which the planets, and we are made. The stars also hint at the immensity of our universe and suggest the vastness of time. The next time you stare into the night sky, consider infinity, consider time, and consider life.

Carinae nebula and stars.